To Garf and 27 wonderful years
of weathering life's storms together xx

– C.A.

To all friends and partners of social movements,
especially the MST in Brazil, who understand that
agroforestry and social justice are the way
to reverse climate change.

– R.D.

First edition published in 2026 Flying Eye Books Ltd.
27 Westgate Street, London, E8 3RL
www.flyingeyebooks.com

Represented by: Abrams & Chronicle Books c/o Media Participations,
57 rue Gaston Tessier, CS 50061, 75166 Paris Cedex 19, France

www.media-participations.com/en/subsidiaries
productsafety@abramsandchronicle.co.uk

Edited by Fay Evans and Maryam Elahi

1 3 5 7 9 10 8 6 4 2

Published in the US by Flying Eye Books Ltd.
Printed in China on FSC® certified paper.

With special thanks to WeatherQuest Ltd

ISBN: 978-1-83874-362-8

MIX
Paper | Supporting responsible forestry
FSC® C137217

Catherine Ard • Rômolo D'Hipólito

EYE OF THE STORM

The Science, Magic, and Meaning of Storms

Flying Eye Books

Contents

ALL ABOUT STORMS

MYTHS AND LEGENDS

STORMS IN THE ARTS

STORMS AND US

ALL ABOUT STORMS

The sky above us may be blue, but at any given moment more than a thousand thunderstorms are rumbling around the world. Hailstones are hammering down, rain is pounding the ground, and powerful gales are blowing.

What Makes the Weather?

The weather is constantly shifting and moving above our heads. It changes with the seasons, from day to day and even by the minute. The temperature, clouds, wind, and rain are all driven by the giant ball of fire in the sky – the Sun.

Heat

The Sun does not warm all the Earth's surface equally. Areas near the equator, around the middle of the planet, are hot because they receive the most heat from the Sun. By the poles, located at the top and bottom of the world, the Sun's rays hit at an angle, making it colder.

Wind

Differences in air temperature create wind. When warm air rises up in areas of low pressure, cold air rushes in to fill its place.

Sea breezes can often cause stronger winds near the coast because the land heats up quicker than water. Warm air above the land rises. Cooler air blows in off the sea to fill the space, creating a breeze.

Air

The Earth is surrounded by a layer of gases, known as the 'atmosphere'. We can't feel it, but the atmosphere is pressing down on us. This is called 'atmospheric pressure'.

Water

Water goes around in an endless cycle. When the Sun heats lakes, rivers, and oceans some water evaporates. It turns into a gas called 'water vapour', which mixes into the air and rises. As it gets higher it cools, and turns back into tiny droplets of liquid. These form clouds.

Droplets swirl around inside a cloud and join together to make big drops.

When droplets become heavy they fall as rain, hail, sleet, or snow. This water collects in rivers, lakes, and oceans, before the cycle starts again.

DID YOU KNOW?

The same water has been on Earth for nearly five billion years, which means that we drink the same water that dinosaurs drank.

Thunder and Lightning

At home you flick a switch to get power, but interestingly electricity also happens in the natural world. A staggering 16 million dramatic thunderstorms crackle and boom around our planet every year!

Colossal clouds

Thunderstorms happen when warm and moist air is allowed to rise rapidly into colder air higher above the ground. This creates towering, dark clouds called 'cumulonimbus'. They can grow up to 10 miles (16 km) high. The air is very cold at this height, and inside the cloud ice crystals form.

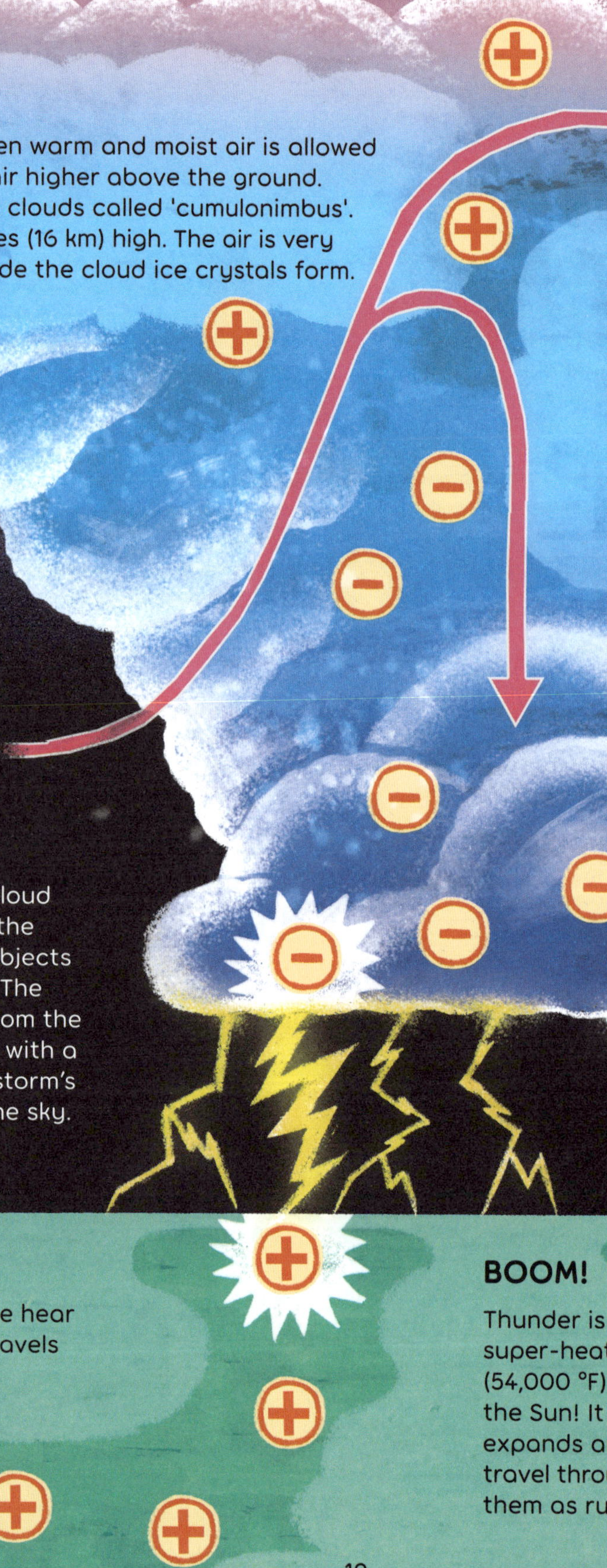

Up and down

The ice crystals are tossed around on currents of rising warm air and sinking cool air. They bump together and charges of static electricity build up. Positive charges on the smaller ice particles move to the top of the cloud and larger hail carrying negative charges sinks to the bottom.

ZAP!

The negative charge in the cloud attracts positive charges in the ground, which move up tall objects like trees towards the cloud. The negative charges descend from the cloud and the currents meet with a flash of lightning. Most of a storm's lightning occurs high up in the sky.

DID YOU KNOW?

We see lightning before we hear thunder because light travels faster than sound.

BOOM!

Thunder is caused because lightning super-heats the air around it to 30,000°C (54,000 °F) – that's five times hotter than the Sun! It happens so fast that the air expands and vibrates. The vibrations travel through the air and our ears hear them as rumbling thunder.

Types of lightning

Cloud-to-cloud

The most common type of lightning. This happens when opposite charges connect inside a cloud or reach another nearby cloud. When this occurs, we see a big sheet of white light known as 'sheet lightning' illuminate the sky.

Cloud-to-air

Some lightning jumps from a cloud into the oppositely charged air around it. This can also appear as sheet lightning.

Ball lightning

This is a rare, currently unexplained form of lightning that forms during or after a thunderstorm. It typically appears near the ground and around power lines, taking the shape of a spherical ball.

Cloud-to-ground

Another common form of lightning that happens when a negative charge in the cloud connects with positively charged ground.

Whirling Winds

Colliding winds and clashing temperatures can create dramatic columns of spinning wind called 'tornadoes'. They travel across the Earth's surface like giant spinning tops, sucking up everything in their path, from cattle to cars.

How a tornado forms

Tornadoes usually begin with a special kind of thunderstorm called a 'supercell'. Supercells also produce hail, strong winds, heavy rain, and lightning.

DID YOU KNOW?

In some places it's raining frogs! Tornadoes and waterspouts sometimes suck up fish and frogs, and then rain them down many miles away.

1. The swirling air sucks in warm air from the ground, this movement is called an 'updraught'. The warm air rises to meet cold air inside the cloud.

2. Stronger winds at different heights within the cloud cause the warm and cold air to spin around each other. This creates a tumbling tube of air, reaching speeds of up to 300 mph (480 kph).

3. If the tumbling tube turns into a vertical column, the storm starts to rotate. This is a supercell.

When a spinning funnel forms below the cloud and reaches the ground, a tornado is born.

Types of Tornado

Waterspouts

These are tornadoes that develop over the sea. A waterspout is not made of water – it is misty air that has descended from a storm cloud, just like a tornado.

Dust devils

These whirling columns of dust and sand form when hot air rises and rotates above dry and dusty landscapes. Although not as powerful as tornadoes, they can reach over a mile (1.6 km) high.

Windy World

A huge storm is brewing far out at sea. From space it looks like a fluffy whirlpool, but down below, the sky turns black and winds whip up wild waves. It is the most violent kind of storm on Earth.

Tropical storms

In different parts of the world, tropical storms are called 'cyclones', 'hurricanes', or 'typhoons', but they all form in the same way. They develop over tropical seas where the air is warm and moist. Seawater evaporates in the Sun, the moist air rises then cools to form storm clouds.

The gathering storm

As the warm, moist air continues to rise, winds begin to spiral, gathering up surrounding thunder clouds. When the spinning winds reach 75 mph (120 kph) the storm has officially become a hurricane.

DID YOU KNOW?

Hurricanes can grow to 10 miles (16 km) high and over 1,000 (1,610 km) wide. The winds can reach 200 miles (322 km) per hour – as fast as a high-speed train or a speeding sportscar.

The eye of the storm

As the storm spins faster and faster, a calm area called the 'eye' develops at the centre. When a hurricane is directly overhead, the fierce wind drops and clouds clear to reveal a sunny, blue sky. Once the eye has passed over, the storm returns with all its force.

Damage and destruction

When a hurricane hits land, it tears through coastal towns and cities, felling trees and flattening buildings. The wind creates pounding waves and pushes seawater onto the shore, flooding the coast. Inland, torrential rain causes landslides and rivers overflow.

In a spin

Storms spin because the Earth is rotating. We can't feel it, but around the middle of the Earth it is spinning at 1,000 mph (1610 kph)! This movement pushes the air in different directions, so that hurricanes north of the equator spin anticlockwise and storms south of the equator spin clockwise.

Death of a storm

As a tropical storm moves over land, it no longer has the heat and moisture from the ocean to power it. It begins to weaken and eventually dies out.

Winter Storms

When temperatures drop, water freezes in clouds, in the air and on the ground. Landscapes turn white as they are battered by hail, smothered by snow, or coated in a slippery layer of ice.

Blizzards

When heavy snow is combined with a strong wind, the air turns white with whirling snowflakes. For a snowstorm to be called a blizzard, each of these things need to happen:

In the UK and the US, the wind speed must be at least 30 miles (48 km) per hour.

Visibility (how far you can see) must be less than 200 metres (656 ft).

The temperature must be freezing or below freezing.

It doesn't need to be snowing for there to be a blizzard. When wind blows fallen snow into the air, there can be a 'ground blizzard.'

Hail

Hail stones are balls of solid ice that form inside thunderclouds. Drops of water freeze as they are pulled high up into the cloud on currents of air. As they are tossed up and down inside the freezing cloud, they collide with water drops and become coated with layers of ice. When the hail becomes heavy it falls to the ground.

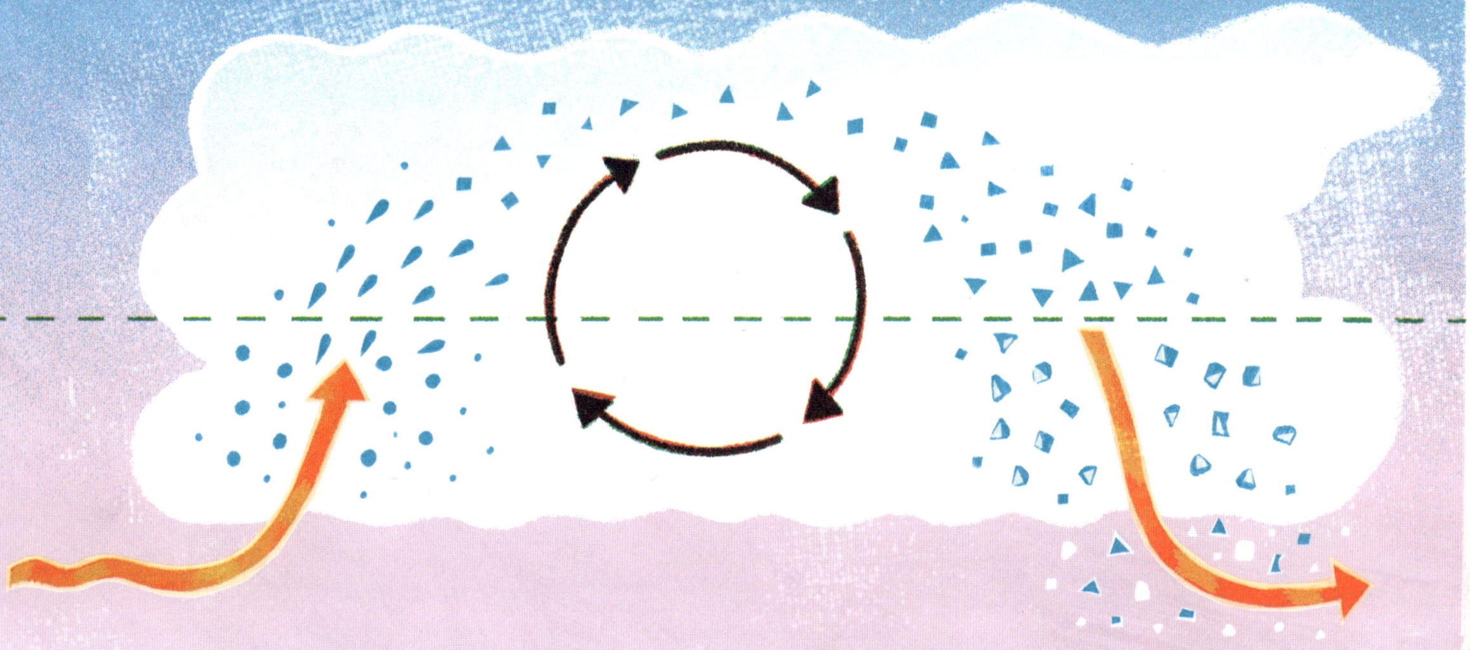

DID YOU KNOW?

Hailstones can be as small as a pea, or as large as a grapefruit! The heaviest hailstones can hit the ground at over 100 miles (160 km) per hour and smash through car windscreens.

Ice storms

Ice storms happen when super-cooled rain freezes as it hits cold surfaces. It surrounds everything in a glaze of slippery ice. When it is thick, the weight of the ice can break tree branches and make electricity cables collapse.

Studying Storms

Scientists called 'meteorologists' study and forecast the weather. They use information gathered on land, at sea, in the sky, and out in space to identify storms and predict where they might strike.

Weather satellites

Weather satellites collect information about cloud temperatures. The information is turned into images that help meteorologists work out where storms might form.

Rockets

Meteorology rockets have instruments in their nosecones that collect information about the atmosphere and wind direction.

Weather balloons

Weather balloons filled with helium rise high into the sky carrying a radiosonde – an instrument that measures conditions in the atmosphere and transmits them back to Earth.

Hurricane hunter planes

Hurricane Hunters are crews of fearless pilots and meteorologists who fly special aircraft straight into the centre of hurricanes. They gather vital information about storms before they hit land.

DID YOU KNOW?

As many as 1,800 weather balloons are launched every day around the world. They drift for hundreds of kilometres before popping and parachuting back down to Earth.

Hurricane buoys

Hurricane buoys bob about on the world's oceans. These floating weather stations are anchored far from land where hurricanes build up. They measure sea and air temperature and the height of waves during storms.

Automatic weather stations

Automatic weather stations gather information on everything from humidity to cloud height. There are more than 10,000 weather stations around the world.

Weather radars

Weather radars scan the skies for severe weather such as tornadoes and thunderstorms. Radars show what kind of weather is happening, from torrential rain to heavy snow. This data can be used to forecast what weather is to come.

Supercomputers

Weather data is put into powerful computers that compare tropical storms in the past to predict how they might develop, and what path they might take in the future.

Tornado chasers

Tornado chasers are scientists who chase storms across the USA in trucks equipped with weather radars. They try to find out more about what causes twisters so they can improve forecasts and warnings.

MYTHS AND LEGENDS

In the past, powerful forces of nature filled people with fear. In many cultures storms were explained in stories about spirits and gods who controlled the weather. The ancient Greeks believed Boreas, the cruel god of the North Wind, brought blizzards and chilled the air with his icy breath.

The Stolen Hammer

The ancient Norse people of Northern Europe worshipped many gods. Thor, the god of thunder, was one of the most powerful. It was said he created violent storms when he rode into battle, and lightning flashed when he threw his mighty hammer.

Daylight robbery

Thor used his hammer to protect the gods and Earth's people from the frost giants. If it landed in the wrong hands, the world would be in danger. One day, Thor put down his heavy weapon and lay down to rest. He drifted off to sleep, and when he awoke his hammer was gone! Bristling with anger, he returned to Asgard, the realm of the gods.

The deal

Loki, god of mischief, offered to investigate. He put on a feathered cloak and flew to Jotunheim, the giants' kingdom. He confronted Thrym, the giant king, who admitted he had stolen the hammer and buried it deep underground where the gods would never find it. The cunning king said he would only return it if the goddess Freya, Thor's stepmother, agreed to marry him.

The plan

Freya refused to marry the giant, and so it was suggested that Thor disguise himself as Freya to trick Thrym. Thor reluctantly agreed to put on a bridal gown and Loki transformed into a bridesmaid to accompany him.

The deception

In the giant's kingdom, Thor hid his face with a bridal veil. Thrym caught a glimpse of Thor's burning eyes beneath the veil, but Loki jumped in to say that Freya was so impatient to be married she had not slept.

The storm

When it was time for the ceremony, the hammer was brought out from its hiding place to make the marriage official. Thor immediately grabbed the weapon and threw back his veil. The air crackled with lightning and the hall shook with thunder as Thor rained down blows on Thrym and his giant family.

DID YOU KNOW?

The name Thor means 'thunder' in the languages spoken by Norse people.

The Power of the Cyclone

Stories passed down by indigenous North Americans tell of powerful spirits who control the wind and storms. The Caddo tribe of Eastern Texas were used to the region's wild weather, and told a story that explained how cyclones came to be.

An unexpected gift

One morning a young boy sat on the riverbank after bathing in the water, when he heard a voice. 'Boy, I know that your grandmother makes you wash all through the winter, no matter how cold, so that you will grow up to be strong. I have come to give you that strength and more power than you ever imagined.'

The power of the cyclone

The boy looked about him, but no one was there. Then he saw an old man rising from the river. 'I am the Power of the Cyclone,' said the old man. He explained that he had once held all the winds in his hands, but now he was old and weak he needed someone to take his place.

Raising the wind

The old man told the boy to lift his arms and swing them. The boy did as he was told, and instantly a black cloud rolled up in the north. 'Swing them faster!' cried the old man. As the boy whirled his arms, a twisting wind descended from the cloud and hit the ground with a terrible roar. It whirled through the trees, tearing them up by their roots.

Stopping in its tracks

'Stand still!' commanded the man. The boy dropped his arms at his sides and the wind stopped as quickly as it had begun. The man told the boy that he had now received his power, and warned never to abuse it, and only send the cyclone in the spring. With that, he disappeared.

Path of the cyclone

The boy became known as 'Path of the Cyclone', and he was both feared and respected by everyone. In the spring, when people saw him swing his arms, they knew that a cyclone would soon follow, and with it bring much-needed rain to water their crops.

DID YOU KNOW?

Florida in the USA is often hit by hurricanes, but for 100 years the city of Tampa has been spared. According to legend, it is protected by an ancient Native American burial mound in the city.

The Slingshot Storm Maker

The Inca people of Peru and South America worshipped the god Illapa, who brought thunder and lightning, hail and rain. Illapa wore golden robes that glittered with precious stones and used a catapult to create storms.

Times of drought

When the fields were parched and the rivers were dry, people would travel into the high mountains with offerings for Illapa and prayers to make it rain.

A cracking shot

Illapa would fill a large clay pot with water from the Milky Way. When the pot was full, he'd fire a stone at it from his slingshot. The stone would then create a roar of thunder as it flew, and when it struck the pot it sent sparks of lightning into the sky.

Let it rain

After the lightning, rain would fall on Earth from the shattered water pot. Illapu was said to care for all animals, so people would attract his attention by tying up black dogs and giving them nothing to eat or drink. Hearing their whining, Illapu would take pity on the dogs and send rain to quench their thirst.

Down to earth

Illapu would sometimes descend to Earth disguised as a puma or a hawk. When he played his pan pipes the trees would come to life and the stones would laugh.

Maui's Kite

Ever since they existed, the islands of Hawaii have been swept by storms that roll in from the Pacific Ocean. There is a legend that tells of the mythical hero, Maui, inventing the kite to harness the wind.

Catching a breeze

One day, Maui decided to create a giant kite. He set to work chopping trees and cutting cloth. But when it was ready there was not a breath of wind, so Maui asked the wise Keeper of the Winds to release some. The woman removed the lid on the magic gourd that contained gentle breezes, and a light wind drifted out and tugged at the kite. It lifted it into the air where it danced above the trees.

Up and away!

Maui was happy, but grew impatient. He wanted his kite to fly as high as the clouds, and asked the wise woman to release the great winds. Despite the Keeper of the Winds warning him that they would be too strong, Maui insisted, reminding her that he was as powerful as any wind. Reluctantly, she took the gourd containing the great winds and lifted the lid.

The wind wins

The winds rushed out at once and ripped the kite from Maui's hands. It soared into the sky and disappeared. Maui tried to call the winds back, but a storm howled and screamed across the land. Palm trees bent in two and heavy rain flooded the fields.

A lesson learned

Eventually, the Keeper of The Winds coaxed them back into the gourd and all was calm. Maui felt humbled. He had learned to treat the wind with respect. He had also learnt that with care the wind could be harnessed, and instead attached a sail to his canoe so he could speed across the sea.

The Boy Lightning and His Mother Thunder

When flashes of lightning slash the dark sky it really does seem like nature is angry. A Nigerian folk tale depicts how a boy made of scorching lightning and his grumbling, thunderous mother became what they are today.

A fiery temper

Long, long ago, thunder and lightning were not found in the sky. They lived on Earth in a village among other people. Lightning was a boy and Thunder was his mother. Lightning had a terrible temper, and often got into arguments with the villagers, and would set light to their houses in anger. Afterwards his mother's scolds echoed through the village.

Royal command

Finally, the village people complained about Lightning to the king, who sent Thunder and her son to live in the forest. Lightning was so furious about being banished that he set fire to the trees. The wind fanned the flames and the fire spread to nearby farms.

Tossed into the sky

The villagers complained again, and the king sent Lightning and Thunder up to the sky where they could not cause any more damage. To this day, Lightning has still not learned his lesson. He sends thunderbolts down to Earth to punish the people who sent him away. His mother can be heard grumbling and scolding him seconds after in her deep, rumbling voice.

Indra Saves the Monsoon

In India, the monsoon season is seen as a gift from the gods. The cool rains bring relief from the stifling summer heat and give life to the parched earth. An ancient story tells of the Hindu god Indra saving the world from drought.

A waterless world

Vritra was a monstrous serpent set upon destroying the world. Its huge scaly body twisted around the whole world, blocking out the Sun and plunging Earth into darkness. It swallowed the streams and rivers, emptied the ocean, dried up all the wells, and sucked every drop of water from the air. The crops were failing and people on Earth were starving.

Warrior to the rescue

People called on the gods for help. They sent the brave and mighty warrior Indra to save the world. Indra rode into the sky on his trusty white elephant, Airavata. He carried his special weapon, a dagger with a jagged blade made of magical material that was as tough as diamonds.

The great battle

Indra was joined by the Maruts, a group of fierce young storm gods. Deafening roars and blinding flashes lit up the sky and the whole world trembled as the two sides clashed. Vritra hissed mist and lashed out with his scaly tail. The battle went on for days, but finally Indra dealt Vritra a fatal blow that pierced his back.

The return of the rains

Vritra cried out as waters came gushing out of his body and fell on the earth. The wells filled up and streams and rivers soon started to flow. Indra had brought back the life-giving rains. The gods crowned him as the King of the Gods, and he has been worshipped ever since.

STORMS IN THE ARTS

When there is a storm brewing in a story or a song, you can be sure something epic is going to happen! Artists and creators have long been captivated by the drama, scale, and spectacle of storms.

Stormy Stories

Writers often use wild weather to communicate the unsettled feelings of their characters. Madness, anger, fear, and passion can all be expressed through howling wind and lashing rain.

Dread and danger

In Herman Melville's epic 1851 adventure *Moby Dick*, captain Ahab becomes dangerously obsessed with killing the gigantic white whale that bit off his leg. A terrible typhoon hits the ship in the Indian Ocean and the crew see it as a bad omen. They want to abandon the mission but Ahab roars at them as the storm rages around them, threatening anyone who does not join him. Ahab should have heeded the warning – Moby Dick wins!

Love and longing

Emily Brontë's 1847 novel *Wuthering Heights* is set on a windswept moor in Yorkshire, England. The stormy weather matches the deep feelings of the characters. Catherine must decide whether to follow her heart and marry the wild and rugged Heathcliff, or settle for rich and respectable Edgar. When she chooses Edgar, a devastated Heathcliff runs away. Catherine is heartbroken and searches for him all night in a violent thunderstorm that nearly kills her.

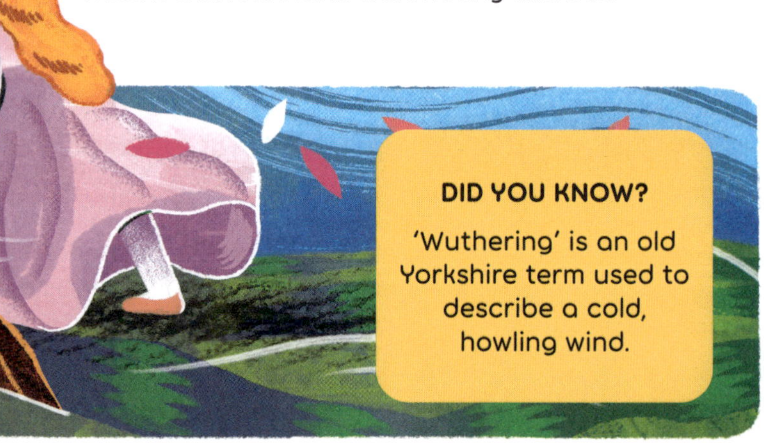

DID YOU KNOW?

'Wuthering' is an old Yorkshire term used to describe a cold, howling wind.

Waves and Woe

William Shakespeare's *The Tempest* (1610–1611) begins with a storm at sea conjured by Prospero, who is marooned on a remote island with his daughter, Miranda. The storm shipwrecks Antonio, Prospero's treacherous brother.

Magic up a Storm

In films, videos, and animations, severe weather can be made to look like it can do anything imaginable. Storms can be summoned up by magic or have the power to transport characters to another world.

Ultimate ice storm

In the 2013 animation *Frozen*, Elsa flees her Scandinavian kingdom so she can unleash her icy powers without harming anyone. As she travels into the mountains, she inadvertently unleashes a blizzard, or ice storm, which brings on an endless winter to the kingdom.

Courage in the storm

In the 2024 animation *Moana 2*, Moana must reach the sunken island of Motufetū to help her own island. However, Motufetū is guarded by the villainous god, Nalo. During the final battle, Nalo creates a menacing storm with huge tornadoes, deadly lightning, and crashing waves to stop Moana from breaking the island's curse.

Blown away

In the 1939 film *The Wizard of Oz*, based on L. Frank Baum's 1900 book, Dorothy's house in Kansas, USA is swept up by a tornado. This causes Dorothy and her dog, Toto to be transported to the magical world of Oz.

DID YOU KNOW?

There were no CGI special effects when *The Wizard of Oz* adaptation was made, so the tornado was created from wire and a 10-metre-long (32 ft) cotton funnel filled with brown dust.

Mastering Storms

Over the centuries, many artists have illustrated the awesome power of storms at sea. They have used different styles and techniques to capture dark and stormy scenes, and real-life stories of danger and destruction.

Nature's might

American painter Georgia O'Keeffe (1887–1986) mostly painted works inspired by nature. In 1922, she painted *A Storm* which she may have witnessed during her time at Lake George, New York. The bright flash of lightning striking the water contrasts beautifully with the dark lake.

Roaring jungle

French painter Henri Rousseau (1844–1910) was most famously known for his jungle paintings, despite never leaving France. While the jungles he painted were imaginary, he drew inspiration from the tropical plants he saw in Paris' botanical gardens. Rousseau painted his first jungle painting in 1891 called *Surprised!* which depicts a tiger lurking in leafy foliage during a raging storm.

Heavenly forces

The original *Wind God and Thunder God* work was painted by Tawaraya Sōtatsu in the 17th century. It was recreated in the early 18th century by Japanese artist Ogata Kōrin (1668–1716). The painting depicts Raijin, the god of thunder, on the left surrounded by small drums which he hits to create storms. Fūjin, the god of wind, is on the right. The gold leaf background can be interpreted as the sky lit up from a lightning strike.

Painting peril

English artist Joseph M. W. Turner (1775–1851) is famous for painting swirling clouds and dangerous seas. In *Snow Storm – Steam-Boat off a Harbour's Mouth* (1842), you can just make out a steamboat being tossed on the waves through a curtain of whirling snow. Turner claimed that he asked sailors to tie him to the mast of the boat as it battled through the waves so that he could experience the storm first hand before he painted it.

DID YOU KNOW?

The 1991 Perfect Storm off the coast of New England, USA and Nova Scotia, Canada sank the fishing vessel, *Andrea Gail*. This incident was dramatised in the 2000 film *The Perfect Storm*, starring George Clooney as the captain of the fishing boat.

Sounding Stormy

Crackles, roars, rumbles, and booms fill the air when a thunderstorm is overhead. Lots of great classical composers have featured Earth's ferocious weather in their works, many of which are considered some of music's most dramatic moments.

Blowing a gale

Italian composer Antonio Vivaldi wrote 'The Storm at Sea' 300 years ago. At that time orchestras were small and there were only a few different types of musical instrument. Vivaldi managed to imitate the sound of a gale using string instruments and the newly invented flute.

Weather-beaten

Ludwig van Beethoven developed ideas during long walks in the countryside. In 1808, he wrote his 'Pastoral Symphony', which tells the story of country folk happily dancing, until they are sent scurrying for cover by a sudden storm. Pounding beats on kettle drums imitate thunderclaps followed by flashes of lightning with sharp cords from violins, cellos, and double bases.

Musical mountain

Richard Strauss wrote 'Thunder and Tempest, An Alpine Symphony' in 1915. He was inspired by a time when he got caught in a downpour while hiking in the Alps as a boy. The musical storm builds to a climax with an orchestra of over 100 musicians creating a noisy turmoil of wild weather. As well as drums, a wind machine and a thunder sheet are used to create a powerful storm.

Stormy sound effects

These special instruments are used to help create realistic storm sounds for orchestral productions.

Snapping Storms

Some of the most awe-inspiring scenes you will ever see form in the skies above us. Storm photographers try to capture the perfect moment when the light, clouds, and wind combine to turn the sky into an enormous canvas of swirling cloud.

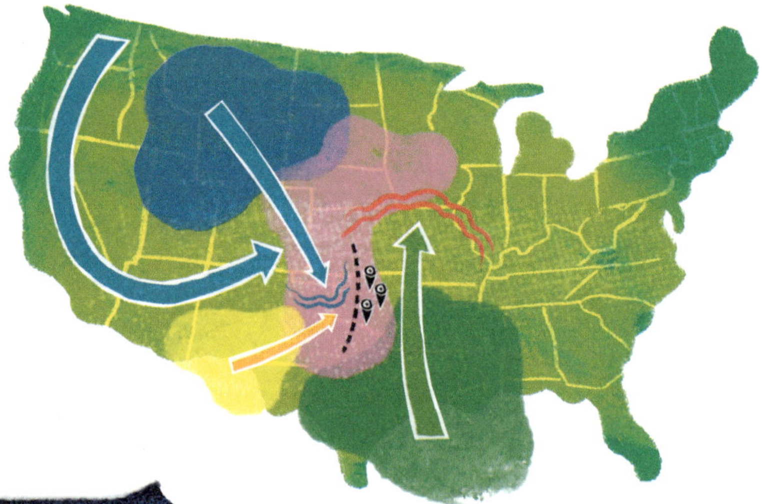

The thrill of the chase

People chase storms in many parts of the world, but the Great Plains of the United States offer ideal conditions. Here, vast flat prairies, good roads, and open skies mix with the frequent formation of huge supercell storms.

Dicing with danger

Storm photographers take calculated risks to snap the best shots. As other people run for cover, they drive directly towards threatening weather fronts. To reduce the danger, they can photograph lightning by setting the camera up on a tripod and triggering it remotely from the safety of their vehicle. They always plan a few escape routes in case the storm suddenly changes speed or direction.

Watching and waiting

Storm photographers need to be experienced in weather forecasting. They study radar images and weather charts to work out where the most dramatic storms will develop. Once they have chosen their destination, they drive vast distances to get into position ahead of the storm. After many hours of waiting and watching the clouds gathering, they may be rewarded with a prize-winning picture.

STORMS AND US

Eight billion people share the planet, but the weather we experience can be vastly different. Some of us will never see a tornado, while others have never witnessed snow. Cool and warm currents of water and air circling the Earth create seasonal storms and localised patterns of extreme weather.

Historical Storms

Imagine winds faster than a high-speed train, and torrential rain that can turn a street into a racing river. When powerful storms make a path for the most populated places on Earth, the effects can be devastating.

Serious snow

The state of New York in the USA often receives heavy snowfall due the 'lake effect'. Cold, dry air from Canada flows across the Great Lakes. Warmth and moisture from the water are picked up and huge snow clouds form. In 1977, a historic snowstorm hit the city of Buffalo on the shores of Lake Eerie. High winds blew snow into 12 metre (40 ft) drifts that buried houses up to their rooves.

Dangerous dust

When strong winds lift dust and sand from deserts, it can be carried for miles. In June 2020, winds whipped up 'Godzilla', the largest dust storm ever recorded in Africa. A gigantic cloud, carrying dust weighing 21 million tonnes (21 billion kg), blew from the Sahara Desert across the Atlantic Ocean to the Caribbean, causing major air pollution.

Terrible tornadoes

About 1,200 tornadoes hit the USA each year. When a group of tornadoes moves along the same path it is called a 'swarm' or 'outbreak'. In 1925, a historically destructive tornado outbreak tore across Missouri, Illinois, and Indiana, named The Tri-State Tornado, destroying thousands of homes along its record-breaking 221 miles (356 km) route.

Killer cyclone

The deadliest tropical cyclone in world history struck Bangladesh in 1970. The Great Bhola Cyclone ripped into the Bay of Bengal with winds of over 125 miles (200 km) per hour. When the sea surged over the flat shoreline at least half a million people lost their lives.

DID YOU KNOW?

Some of the biggest hailstorms in the world occur in hot climates. The heaviest hailstones ever recorded fell in Bangladesh on April 14, 1986. Some weighed as much as a pineapple!

Living with Storms

Each year, 80 to 90 tropical storms form over the world's warm oceans. Over half of these develop into hurricanes, the most powerful and destructive weather events on the planet.

The strength of storms

Hurricanes (also known as cyclones or typhoons) are given a category rating from one to five, which estimates how much damage they will cause.

CATEGORY 1

Winds 74-95 mph (119-153 km/h)
Some damage and power cuts

CATEGORY 2

Winds 96-110 mph (154-177 km/h)
Extensive damage

CATEGORY 3

Winds 111-129 mph (178-208 km/h)
Well-built homes suffer major damage

CATEGORY 4

Winds 130-156 mph (209-251 km/h)
Severe damage to well-built homes

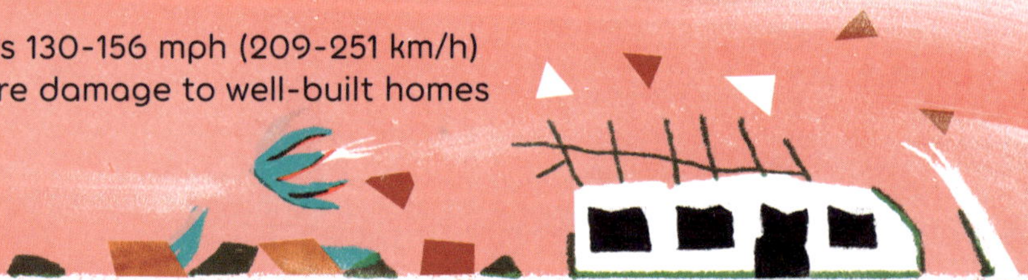

CATEGORY 5

Winds 157+ mph (252+ km/h)
Many buildings destroyed, major roads cut off

Hurricane hazards

Hurricanes are known for their violent winds, but the greatest threats they bring actually come from water.

High tides

When hurricane-force winds push the sea up and over the shore it is called a 'storm surge'. The water level can rise up to eight metres (26 feet) above normal – as tall as a telephone pole – and floods in over the land for several miles, damaging crops and property and even destroying lives.

Hazardous seas

The strong winds of a tropical cyclone can cause huge waves that batter the coast and wreck ships out at sea, even when a storm is far from land. These waves can create dangerous rip currents where water flows away from the shore, pulling even the strongest swimmers out to sea.

Heavy rain

Hurricanes bring heavy rain that can last for several days after the storm has passed. Rivers burst their banks, bridges and roads are washed away and land and homes are flooded for hundreds of miles around.

The Coming Storm

Meteorologists use technology to monitor storms and predict where and when they will hit land. Nothing can stop a hurricane that is heading for the coast, but there are plenty of ways to prepare for it.

Storm names

Every hurricane is given a name to make it easier to communicate information about it to the public. Different areas of the world have their own lists of names. In the western North Pacific and North Indian Ocean regions storms are named after flowers, animals, birds, trees, and foods.

Storm warnings

Information about an approaching hurricane is sent out in lots of different ways. Storm reports are broadcast on television and radio stations. Websites and weather apps give up-to-the-minute information and some governments send emergency alerts to people's mobile phones. Warning flags are raised along coasts to alert ships and local residents.

DID YOU KNOW?

English naval officer Robert Fitzroy started the world's first national storm warning service after the Royal Charter Gale of 1859, which took 800 lives and sunk 133 boats and ships in the Irish Sea.

Getting ready

Once the news of an approaching hurricane is spread, people start making preparations.

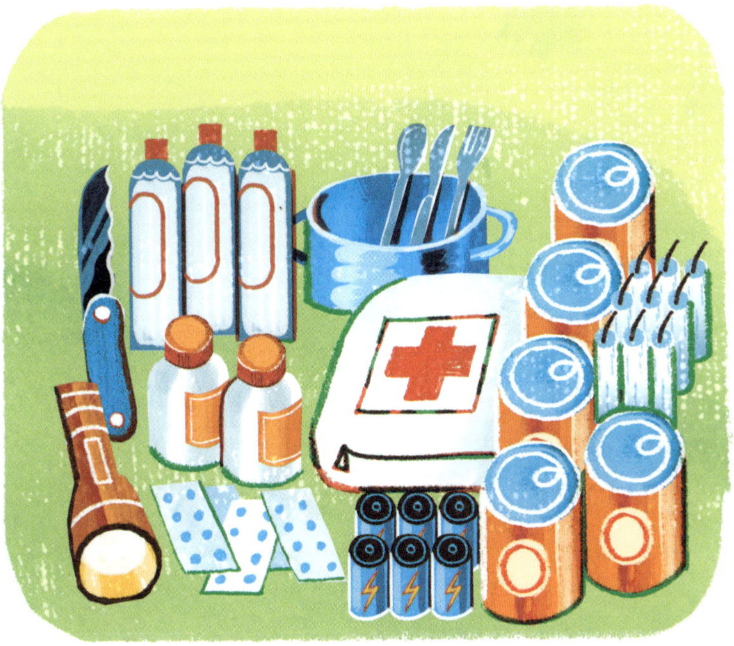

Emergency kit

When the storm arrives, the power and water supply may be cut. A kit containing food, drinking water, torches, batteries, and first aid items needs to be gathered.

Secure property

Hurricane-force winds can shatter windows and hurl heavy objects through the air. Rubbish bins and garden furniture need to be taken inside. Doors and windows must be covered with shutters or boarded up.

Another place

People living directly in the storm's path may be told to evacuate. They leave their homes and head to a safer area.

Safe space

People and their pets must shelter inside during the storm. A room away from windows such as a hallway or basement offers good protection.

Building for Storms

Around the world, engineers and architects have come up with incredible solutions to protect land and communities from the destruction caused by storms.

Hold back the tide

In 1953, a storm in the North Sea caused a tidal surge that killed over two thousand people in the Netherlands, Belgium, England, and Scotland. After this, work began to stop this from ever happening again.

The Netherlands built the Delta Works – the world's biggest flood protection system. It is made up of 13 gates, damns, and barriers that stop the sea flooding across the country's low, flat lands. The Maeslant Barrier is a flood and storm surge barrier and the largest moveable object on the planet! Each gate is 210 metres (670 ft) wide – more than the length of three passenger planes.

The Thames Barrier (completed in 1982) was built across the river Thames in London, England. It protects about 1.4 million people in the capital city when storm surges sweep up the river. 10 enormous steel gates, the height of a five-storey building, hold back the water.

Go with the flow

Buildings can be cleverly designed to stand strong while the storm rages on.

Many tropical countries, such as Thailand and Vietnam, build houses on stilts. During storms and heavy rains families stay safe and dry while the floodwater flows underneath.

In the Netherlands, many people live in floating homes. Houses are built on floating platforms, so they rise up with the water.

Dome homes are built in hurricane hot spots, like Florida in the USA. The arched buildings are made with strong concrete and steel. Their curved shape allows wind to flow smoothly over and around them.

A Stormy Future

Our planet is getting warmer, and many scientists believe that this is affecting all sorts of weather, including storms. Hurricanes, typhoons, and cyclones are not happening more often, but they seem to be getting more powerful.

A warmer, wetter planet

Hurricanes suck up hot, moist air from tropical oceans. Warmer ocean waters mean storms can pick up more energy, leading to higher wind speeds.

More heat from the sun is trapped within our atmosphere, causing more water to evaporate. The moisture forms clouds, which bring heavier rainfall.

The glaciers and ice sheets at the North and South Poles are melting, which is making the sea levels rise. This makes flooding worse when there are storm surges.

Surprising storms

It is becoming harder for meteorologists to predict what hurricanes will do. Although forecasting systems are improving, global warming is causing more storms to strengthen quickly and change their path before they strike land. Storms may be stronger, but they can also hold more water and last for longer, bringing longer periods of heavy rain.

Taking action

World governments are taking steps to protect the planet. Fossil fuels are being replaced with cleaner options such as wind, wave, and solar power. More and more cars and buses are powered by electricity, and people are finding ways to reduce the energy they use.

Glossary

Atmosphere – a layer of gasses, like nitrogen, oxygen, and carbon dioxide, that surround the Earth. It keeps us warm, gives us air to breathe, and blocks harmful rays from the sun.

Equator – an imaginary line around the middle of the Earth that divides it into the Northern and Southern Hemisphere. Countries near the equator are usually hot and have lots of rain, because the sun shines almost directly on them all year round.

Evacuation – leaving a place due to storms, floods, fires, or other emergencies to go somewhere safe until the danger is gone.

Evaporation – the process whereby a liquid changes into a gas, particularly by being heated.

Fossil fuels – are formed over millions of years from decomposing plants and organisms. The three main fossil fuels are coal, oil, and natural gas which we burn for fuel.

Gale – a very strong wind.

Glacier – a huge mass of ice that forms from lots of packed snow over many years. They are found in very cold places, like the Arctic, Antarctica, and high mountain regions.

Hurricane – a huge, powerful storm with very strong winds that can cause heavy rain and even flooding. They form over warm ocean waters and can grow to be hundreds of miles wide.

Humid – when the air has a high level of water vapour.

Index

Landslides – occur when rocks and soil slide down a hill or mountain often after heavy rain or an earthquake.

Lightning – a powerful flash of electricity that happens during a storm and is hotter than the surface of the Sun.

Meteorologist – a scientist who studies the weather.

Supercell – a type of thunderstorm with a rotating updraught. It can last for several hours and bring severe weather such as strong winds, heavy rain, hail, and flooding.

Mist – a cloud of water droplets in the air.

The Great Plains – a large, flat area of land in the middle of North America. It's often called 'America's breadbasket' as crops like wheat and corn are grown there.

Thunder – the loud sound caused by the extreme heat of a flash of lightning during a storm. The sound arrives after the flash because light travels faster.

Tidal surge – occurs when strong winds and low air pressure from a storm push ocean water onto land. Also known as a 'storm surge'.

Tornado – A rapidly spinning column of air that stretches from a storm cloud down to the ground. Also known as a 'twister'.

Torrential rain – very heavy rain that falls fast and hard.

Water vapour – water in the form of an invisible gas. Water vapour is part of the air we breathe and helps form clouds, rain, and snow.